D1607479

ISBN 978-0-265-40404-1
PIBN 10237454

The Broken Wing

e Bro en Wing
Songs of Love, Death & Destiny
1915–1916

By Sarojini Naidu

Author of
" The Golden Threshold " " The Bird of Time "

London : William Heinemann
New York : John Lane Company
1917

Dedication

To the Dream of To-day

and

The Hope of To-morrow

HYDERABAD, DECCAN
August 10, 1916

Foreword

In the radiant and far-off yesterdays of our history it was the sacred duty of Indian womanhood to kindle and sustain the hearth-fires, the beacon-fires, and the altar-fires of the nation.

The Indian woman of to-day is once more awake and profoundly alive to her splendid destiny as the guardian and interpreter of the Triune Vision of national life—the Vision of Love, the Vision of Faith, the Vision of Patriotism.

Her renascent consciousness is everywhere striving for earnest expression in song or speech, service or self-sacrifice, that shall prove an offering not unworthy of the Great Mother in the eyes of the world that honour her.

Poignantly aware of the poverty of my gift, I still venture to make my offering with joined palms uplifted in a Salutation of Song.

SAROJINI NAIDU

HYDERABAD, DECCAN, 1916

I offer all due acknowledgments to the editors of
the various European and Oriental journals in
which my poems have appeared.

Contents

c

The Flowering Year

The Peacock Lute : Songs for Music

The Temple : A Pilgrimage of Love

The Broken Wing
Songs of Life and Death

The Broken Wing

"Why should a song-bird like you have a broken wing?"
G. K. GOKHALE

QUESTION

THE great dawn breaks, the mournful night is past,
From her deep age-long sleep she wakes at last !
Sweet and long-slumbering buds of gladness ope
Fresh lips to the returning winds of hope,
Our eager hearts renew their radiant flight
Towards the glory of renascent light,
Life and our land await their destined spring . . .
Song-bird why dost *thou* bear a broken wing ?

ANSWER

Shall spring that wakes mine ancient land again
. Call to my wild and suffering heart in vain ?
Or Fate's blind arrows still the pulsing note
Of my far-reaching, frail, unconquered throat ?

Or a weak bleeding pinion daunt or tire
My flight to the high realms of my desire ?
Behold ! I rise to meet the destined spring
And scale the stars upon my broken wing !

The Gift of India

Is there aught you need that my hands withhold,
Rich gifts of raiment or grain or gold?
Lo! I have flung to the East and West
Priceless treasures torn from my breast,
And yielded the sons of my stricken womb
To the drum-beats of duty, the sabres of doom.

Gathered like pearls in their alien graves
Silent they sleep by the Persian waves,
Scattered like shells on Egyptian sands,
They lie with pale brows and brave, broken hands,
They are strewn like blossoms mown down by chance
On the blood-brown meadows of Flanders and France.

Can ye measure the grief of the tears I weep
Or compass the woe of the watch I keep?

Or the pride that thrills thro' my heart's despair,
And the hope that comforts the anguish of prayer?
And the far sad glorious vision I see
Of the torn red banners of Victory?

When the terror and tumult of hate shall cease
And life be refashioned on anvils of peace,
And your love shall offer memorial thanks
To the comrades who fought in your dauntless ranks,
And you honour the deeds of the deathless ones
Remember the blood of thy martyred sons!

August 1915

The Temple ∠

Awake, it is Love's radiant hour of praise !
Bring new-blown leaves his temple to adorn,
Pomegranate-buds and ripe sirisha-sprays,
Wet sheaves of shining corn.

PILGRIM

O priest ! only my broken lute I bring
For Love's praise-offering !

PRIEST

Behold ! the hour of sacrifice draws near.
Pile high the gleaming altar-stones of Love
With, delicate burdens of slain woodland deer
And frail white mountain dove.

PILGRIM

O·priest ! only my wounded heart I bring
For Love's blood-offering !

PRIEST

Lo ! now it strikes Love's solemn hour of prayer,
Kindle with fragrant boughs his blazing shrine,
Feed the sweet flame with spice and incense rare,
Curds of rose-pastured kine.

PILGRIM

O·priest ! only my stricken soul I bring
For Love's burnt-offering !

Lakshmi, the Lotus-Born

Goddess of Fortune

Thou who didst rise like a pearl from the ocean,
Whose beauty surpasseth the splendour of morn!
Lo! We invoke thee with eager devotion,
      Hearken, O Lotus-born!

Come! with sweet eyelids and fingers caressing,
With footfalls auspicious our thresholds adorn,
And grant us the showers and the sheaves of thy
      blessing,
      Hearken, O Lotus-born!

Prosper our cradles and kindred and cattle,
And cherish our hearth-fires and coffers and corn,
O watch o'er our seasons of peace and of battle,
      Hearken, O Lotus-born!

For our dear Land do we offer oblation,
O keep thou her glory unsullied, unshorn,
And guard the invincible hope of our nation,
Hearken, O Lotus-born !

Lakshmi Puja Day, 1915

The Victor

THEY brought their peacock-lutes or praise
And carven gems in jasper trays,
Rich stores of fragrant musk and myrrh,
And wreaths of scarlet nenuphar . . .
I had no offering that was meet,
And bowed my face upon his feet.

They brought him robes from regal looms,
Inwrought with pearl and silver blooms,
And sumptuous footcloths broiderèd
With beetle-wings and gleaming thread . . .
I had no offering that was meet,
And spread my hands beneath his feet.

They filled his courts with gifts of price,
With tiers of grain and towers of spice,

Tall jars of golden oil and wine,
And heads of camel and of kine . . .
I had no offering that was meet,
And laid my life before his feet.

The Imam Bara

I

Out of the sombre shadows,
Over the sunlit grass,
Slow in a sad procession
The shadowy pageants pass
Mournful, majestic, and solemn,
Stricken and pale and dumb,
Crowned in their peerless anguish
The sacred martyrs come.
Hark, from the brooding silence
Breaks the wild cry of pain
Wrung from the heart of the ages
   Ali ! Hassan ! Hussain !

II

Come from this tomb of shadows,
Come from this tragic shrine
That throbs with the deathless sorrow
Of a long-dead martyr line.
Love ! let the living sunlight
Kindle your splendid eyes
Ablaze with the steadfast triumph
Of the spirit that never dies.
So may the hope of new ages
Comfort the mystic pain
That cries from the ancient silence
    Ali ! Hassan ! Hussain !

The Imam Bara is a Chapel of Lamentation where Mussulmans of the Shiah Community celebrate the tragic martyrdom of Ali, Hassan, and Hussain during the mourning month of Moharram. A sort of passion-play takes place to the accompaniment of the refrain, Ali ! Hassan ! Hussain !

A Song from Shiraz

THE singers of Shiraz are feasting afar
To greet the Nauraz with sarang and cithar. . . .
But what is their music that calleth to me,
From glimmering garden and glowing minar?

The stars shall be scattered like jewels of glass,
And Beauty be tossed like a shell in the sea,
Ere the lutes of their magical laughter surpass
The lutes of thy tears, O Mohamed Ali!

From the Mosque-towers of Shiraz ere daylight begin
My heart is disturbed by the loud muezzin,
But what is the voice of his warning to me,
That waketh the world to atonement of sin?

The stars shall be broken like mirrors of brass,
And Rapture be sunk like a stone in the sea,
Ere the carpet of·prayer or of·penance surpass
Thy carpet of dreams, O Mohamed Ali!

In the silence of Shiraz my soul shall await,
Untroubled, the wandering Angel of Fate. . . .
What terror or joy shall his hands hold for me,
Who bringeth the goblet of guerdon too late?

The stars shall be mown and uprooted like grass,
And Glory be flung like a weed in the sea,
Ere the goblet of doom or salvation surpass
Thy goblet of love, O Mohamed Ali!

Imperial Delhi

IMPERIAL City ! dowered with sovereign grace
To thy renascent glory still there clings
The splendid tragedy of ancient things,
The regal woes of many a vanquished race ;
And memory's tears are cold upon thy face
E'en while thy heart's returning gladness rings
Loud on the sleep of thy forgotten kings,
Who in thine arms sought Life's last resting-place.

Thy changing kings and kingdoms pass away
The gorgeous legends of a bygone day,
But thou dost still immutably remain
Unbroken symbol of proud histories,
Unageing priestess of old mysteries
Before whose shrine the spells of Death are vain.

1912

Memorial Verses
I. Ya Mahbub !*

ARE these the streets that I used to know—
Was it yesterday or æons ago ?
Where are the armies that used to wait—
The pilgrims of Love—at your palace gate ?
The joyous pæans that thrilled the air
The pageants that shone thro' your palace square ?
And the minstrel music that used to ring
Thro' your magic kingdom . . . when you were
    king ?

O hands that succoured a people's need
With the splendour of Haroun-al-Rasheed !

* " Ya Mahbub," which means O Beloved, 'twas
the device on the State banner of the late Nizam
of Hyderabad, Mir Mahbub Ali Khan, the well-
beloved of his people.

O heart that solaced a sad world's cry
With the sumptuous bounty of Hatim Tai !
Where are the days that were winged and clad
In the fabulous glamour of old Baghdad,
And the bird of glory that used to sing
In your magic kingdom . . . when you were king ?

O king, in your kingdom there is no change.
'Tis only my soul that hath grown so strange,
So faint with sorrow it cannot hear
Aught save the chant at your rose-crowned bier.
My grieving bosom hath grown too cold
To clasp the beauty it treasured of old,
The grace of life and the gifts of spring,
And the dreams I cherished . . . when you were
    king !

August 29, 1911

II. Gokhale *

HEROIC Heart ! lost hope of all our days !
Need'st thou the homage of our love or praise ?
Lo ! let the mournful millions round thy pyre
Kindle their souls with consecrated fire
Caught from the brave torch fallen from thy hand,
To succour and to serve our suffering land
And in a daily worship taught by thee
Upbuild the temple of her Unity.

February 19, 1915

* *Gopal Krishna Gokhale, the great saint and soldier of our national righteousness. His life was a sacrament, and his death was a sacrifice in the cause of Indian unity.*

20

In Salutation to my Father's Spirit ✔

Aghorenath Chattopadhyay

FAREWELL, farewell, O brave and tender Sage.
O mystic jester, golden-hearted Child !
Selfless, serene, untroubled, unbeguiled
By trivial snares of grief and greed or rage ;
O splendid dreamer in a dreamless age
Whose deep alchemic vision reconciled
Time's changing message with the undefiled
Calm wisdom of thy Vedic heritage !

Farewell great spirit, without rear or flaw,
Thy life was love and liberty thy law,
And Truth thy pure imperishable goal . . .
All hail to thee in thy transcendent flight
From hope to hope, from height to heav'nlier height,
Lost in the rapture of the Cosmic Soul.

January 28, 1915

The Flute-Player of Brindaban *

WHY didst thou play thy matchless flute
    Neath the Kadamba tree,
And wound my idly dreaming heart
    With poignant melody,
So where thou goest I must go,
    My flute-player, with thee ?

Still must I like a homeless bird
    Wander, forsaking all ;
The earthly loves and worldly lures
    That held my life in thrall,
And follow, follow, answering
    Thy magical flute-call.

* *Krishna, the Divine Flute-player of Brindaban,
who plays the tune of the Infinite that lures every
Hindu heart away from mortal cares and attachments.*

To Indra's golden-flowering groves
    Where streams immortal flow,
Or to sad Yama's silent Courts
    Engulfed in lampless woe,
Where'er thy subtle flute I hear
    Belovèd I must go !

No peril of the deep or height
    Shall daunt my wingèd foot ;
No fear of time-unconquered space,
    Or light untravelled route,
Impede my heart that pants to drain
    The nectar of thy flute !

Farewell

FAREWELL, O eager faces that surround me,
Claiming the tender service of my days,
Farewell, O joyous spirits that have bound me
With the love-sprinkled garlands of your praise !

O golden lamps of hope how shall I bring you
Life's kindling flame from a forsaken fire ?
O glowing hearts of youth, how shall I sing you
Life's glorious message from a broken lyre ?

To you what further homage shall I render,
Victorious City girdled by the sea,
Where breaks in surging tides of woe and splendour
The age-long tumult of Humanity ?

Need you another tribute for a token
Who reft from me the pride of all my years ?
Lo ! I will leave you with farewell unspoken,
Shrine of dead dream ! O temple of my tears !

The Challenge

Thou who dost quell in thy victorious tide
Death's ravaged secret and life's ruined pride,
Shall thy great deeps prevail, O conquering Sea,
O'er Love's relentless tides of memory ?

Sweet Earth, though in thy lustrous bowl doth shine
The limpid flame of hope's perennial wine,
Thou art too narrow and too frail to bear
The harsh, wild vintage of my heart's despair.

O valiant skies, so eager to uphold
High laughing burdens of sidereal gold,
Swift would your brave brows perish to sustain
The radiant silence of my sleepless pain.

Wandering Beggars

FROM the threshold of the Dawn
On we wander, always on
Till the friendly light be gone
  Y' Allah ! Y' Allah !

We are free-born sons of Fate,
What care we for wealth or state
Or the glory of the great ?
  Y' Allah ! Y' Allah !

Life may grant us or withhold
Roof or raiment, bread or gold,
But our hearts are gay and bold.
  Y' Allah ! Y' Allah !

Time is like a wind that blows,
The future is a folded rose,
Who shall pluck it no man knows.
   Y' Allah ! Y' Allah !

So we go a fearless band,
The staff of freedom in our hand
Wandering from land to land,
   Y' Allah ! Y' Allah !

Till we meet the Night that brings
Both to beggars and to kings
The end of all their journeyings
   Y' Allah ! Y' Allah !

The Lotus

To M. K. Gandhi

O MYSTIC Lotus, sacred and sublime,
In myriad-petalled grace inviolate,
Supreme o'er transient storms of tragic Fate,
Deep-rooted in the waters of all Time,
What legions loosed from many a far-off clime
Of wild-bee hordes with lips insatiate,
And hungry winds with wings of hope or hate,
Have thronged and pressed round thy miraculous prime
To devastate thy loveliness, to drain
The midmost rapture of thy glorious heart . . .
But who could win thy secret, who attain
Thine ageless beauty born of Brahma's breath,
Or pluck thine immortality, who art
Coeval with the Lords of Life and Death?

The Prayer of Islam

WE praise Thee, O Compassionate !
Master of Life, and Time and Fate,
Lord of the labouring winds and seas,
    Ya Hameed ! Ya Hafeez !

Thou art the Radiance of our ways,
Thou art the Pardon of our days,
Whose name is known from star to star,
    Ya Ghani ! Ya Ghaffar !

Thou art the Goal for which we long,
Thou art our Silence and our Song,
Life of the sunbeam and the seed—
    Ya Wahab ! Ya Waheed !

Thou dost transmute from hour to hour
Our mortal weakness into power,
Our bondage into liberty,
    Ya Quadeer ! Ya Quavi !

We are the shadows of Thy Light,
We are the secrets of Thy might,
The visions of thy primal dream,
    Ya Rahman ! Ya Raheem ! *

    Id-uz-Zoha, 1915

---

* *These are some of the Ninety-nine Beautiful Arabic Names of God as used by followers of Islam.*

Bells

Anklet-bells

ANKLET-BELLS ! frail anklet-bells !
That hold Love's ancient mystery
As hide the lips of limpid shells
Faint tones of the remembered sea,
You murmur of enchanted rites,
Of sobbing breath and broken speech,
Sweet anguish of rose-scented nights
And wild mouths calling each to each
Or mute with yearning ecstasy.

Cattle-bells

Cattle-bells ! soft cattle-bells !
What gracious memories you bring
Of drowsy fields and dreaming wells,

32

And weary labour's folded wing,
Of frugal mirth round festal fires,
Brief trysts that youth and beauty keep.
Of flowering roofs and fragrant byres
White heifers gathered in for sleep,
Old songs the wandering women sing.

Temple-bells

Temple-bells ! deep temple-bells !
Whose urgent voices wreck the sky !
In your importunate music dwells
Man's sad and immemorial cry
That cleaves the dawn with wings of praise,
That cleaves the dark with wings of prayer,
Craves pity for our mortal ways,
Seeks solace for our life's despair,
And peace for suffering hearts that die !

The Garden Vigil

In the deep silence of the garden-bowers
Only the stealthy zephyr glides and goes,
Rifling the secret of *sirisha* flowers,
And to the new-born hours
Bequeathes the subtle anguish of the rose.

Pain-weary and dream-worn I lie awake,
Counting like beads the blazing stars o'erhead;
Round me the wind-stirred champak branches shake
Blossoms that fall and break
In perfumed rain across my lonely bed.

Long ere the sun's first far-off beacons shine,
Or her prophetic clarions call afar,
The gorgeous planets wither and decline,—
Save in its eastern shrine,
Unquenched, unchallenged, the proud morning star.

34

O glorious light of hope beyond all reach !
O lovely symbol and sweet sign of him
Whose voice I yearn to hear in tender speech
To comfort me or teach,
Before whose gaze thy golden fires grow dim !

I care not what brave splendours bloom or die
So thou dost burn in thine appointed place,
Supreme in the still dawn-uncoloured sky,
And daily grant that I
May in thy flame adore his hidden face.

Invincible

O FATE, betwixt the grinding-stones of Pain,
Tho' you have crushed my life like broken grain,
Lo ! I will leaven it with my tears and knead
The bread of Hope to comfort and to feed
The myriad hearts for whom no harvests blow
    Save bitter herbs of woe.

Tho' in the flame of sorrow you have thrust
My flowering soul and trod it into dust,
Behold, it doth reblossom like a grove
To shelter under quickening boughs of Love
The myriad souls for whom no gardens bloom
    Save bitter buds of doom.

The Pearl

How long shall it suffice
    Merely to hoard in thine unequalled rays
  The bright sequestered colours of the sun,
O pearl above all price,
    And beautiful beyond all need of praise,
  World-coveted but yet possessed of none,
  Content in thy proud self-dominion ?

Shall not some ultimate
    And unknown hour deliver thee, and attest
  Life's urgent and inviolable claim
To bind and consecrate
    Thy glory on some pure and bridal breast,
  Or set thee to enhance with flawless flame
  A new-born nation's coronal of fame ?

Or wilt thou self-denied
        Forgo such sweet and sacramental ties
    As weld Love's delicate bonds of ecstasy,
And in a barren pride
        Of cold, unfruitful freedom that belies
    The inmost secret of fine liberty
    Return unblest into the primal sea ?

Three Sorrows

How shall I honour thee, O sacred grief?
Fain would my love transmute
My suffering into music and my heart
Into a deathless lute !

How shall I cherish thee, O precious pain ?
Fain would my trembling hand
Fashion and forge of thee a deathless sword
To serve my stricken land !

And thou, sweet sorrow, terrible and dear,
Most bitter and divine ?
O I will carve thee with deep agony
Into a deathless shrine !

Kali the Mother

All Voices :   O TERRIBLE and tender and divine !
O mystic mother of all sacrifice,
We deck the sombre altars of thy shrine
With sacred basil leaves and saffron
rice ;
All gifts of life and death we bring to
thee,
Uma Haimavati !

Maidens :   We bring thee buds and berries from
the wood !

Brides :   We bring the rapture of our bridal
prayer !

Mothers :   And we the sweet travail of mother-
hood !

Widows :	And we the bitter vigils of despair !
All Voices :	All gladness and all grief we bring to thee, *Ambika ! Parvati !*
Artisans :	We bring the lowly tribute of our toil !
Peasants :	We bring our new-born goats and budded wheat !
Victors :	And we the swords and symbols of our spoil !
Vanquished :	And we the shame and sorrow of defeat !
All Voices :	All triumph and all tears we bring to thee, *Girija ! Shambhavi !*
Scholars :	We bring the secrets of our ancient arts.
Priests :	We bring the treasures of our ageless creeds.
Poets :	And we the subtle music of our hearts.

41

Patriots :   And we the sleepless worship of our deeds.

All Voices :   All glory and all grace we bring to thee, *Kali ! Maheshwari ! **

* *These are some of the many name Eternal Mother of Hindu worship.*

Awake ! * ⌣

To Mohamed Ali Jinnah

WAKEN, O mother ! thy children implore thee,
Who kneel in thy presence to serve and adore thee !
The night is aflush with a dream of the morrow,
Why still dost thou sleep in thy bondage of sorrow ?
Awaken and sever the woes that enthral us,
And hallow our hands for the triumphs that call us !

Are we not thine, O Belov'd, to inherit
The manifold pride and power of thy spirit ?
Ne'er shall we fail thee, forsake thee or falter,
Whose hearts are thy home and thy shield and thine
      altar.
Lo ! we would thrill the high stars with thy story,
And set thee again in the forefront of glory.

* *Recited at the Indian National Congress, 1915.*

43

Hindus :	Mother ! the flowers of our worship have crowned thee !
Parsees :	Mother ! the flame of our hope shall surround thee !
Mussulmans :	Mother ! the sword of our love shall defend thee !
Christians :	Mother ! the song of our faith shall attend thee !
All Creeds :	Shall not our dauntless devotion avail thee ? Hearken ! O queen and O goddess, we hail thee !

The Flowering Year

" A light of laughing flowers along the grass is spread "
SHELLEY

The Call of Spring

To Padmaja and Lilamani

CHILDREN, my children, the spring wakes anew,
And calls through the dawn and the daytime
For flower-like and fleet-footed maidens like you,
To share in the joy of its playtime.

O'er hill-side and valley, through garden and grove,
Such exquisite anthems are ringing
Where rapturous bulbul and maina and dove
Their carols of welcome are singing.

I know where the ivory lilies unfold
In brooklets half-hidden in sedges,
And the air is aglow with the blossoming gold
Of thickets and hollows and hedges.

I know where the dragon-flies glimmer and glide,
And the plumes of wild peacocks are gleaming,
Where the fox and the squirrel and timid fawn hide
And the hawk and the heron lie dreaming.

The earth is ashine like a humming-bird's wing,
And the sky like a kingfisher's feather,
O come, let us go and play with the spring
Like glad-hearted children together.

The Coming of Spring

O SPRING! I cannot run to greet
    Your coming as I did of old,
    Clad in a shining veil of gold,
With champa-buds and blowing wheat
And silver anklets on my feet.

Let others tread the flowering ways
    And pluck new leaves to bind their brows,
    And swing beneath the quickening boughs
A bloom with scented spikes and sprays
Of coral and of chrysoprase.

But ir against this sheltering wall
    I lean to rest and lag behind,
    Think not my love untrue, unkind,
Or heedless of the luring call
To your enchanting festival.

O Sweet ! I am not false to you—
    Only my weary heart of late
    Has fallen from its high estate
Of laughter and has lost the clue
To all the vernal joy it knew.

There was a song I used to sing—
    But now I seek in vain, in vain
    For the old lilting glad refrain—
I have forgotten everything—
Forgive me, O my comrade Spring !

Vasant Panchami Day, 1916

The Magic of Spring

I BURIED my heart so deep, so deep,
Under a secret hill of pain,
And said, " O broken pitiful thing
Even the magic spring
Shall ne'er awake thee to life again,
Tho' March woods glimmer with opal rain
And passionate koels sing."

The kimshuks burst into dazzling flower,
The seemuls burgeoned in crimson pride,
The palm-groves shone with the oriole's wing,
The koels began to sing,
And soft clouds broke in a twinkling tide . . .
My heart leapt up in its grave and cried,
" *Is it the spring, the spring ?* "

Summer Woods

O I AM tired of painted roofs and soft and silken
    floors,
And long for wind-blown canopies of crimson *gul-*
    mohurs !

O I am tired of strife and song and festivals and
    fame,
And long to fly where cassia-woods are breaking into
    flame.

Love, come with me where koels call from flowering
    glade and glen,
Far from the toil and weariness, the praise and prayers
    of men.

O let us fling all care away, and lie alone and dream
'Neath tangled boughs of tamarind and *molsari* and
   neem !

And bind our brows with jasmine sprays and play
   on carven flutes,
To wake the slumbering serpent-kings among the
   banyan roots,

And roam at fall of eventide along the river's brink,
And bathe in water-lily pools where golden panthers
   drink !

You and I together, Love, in the deep blossoming
   woods
Engirt with low-voiced silences and gleaming soli-
   tudes,

Companions of the lustrous dawn, gay comrades of
   the night,
Like Krishna and like Radhika, encompassed with
   delight.

June Sunset

HERE shall my heart find its haven of calm,
By rush-fringed rivers and rain-fed streams
That glimmer thro' meadows of lily and palm.
Here shall my soul find its true repose
Under a sunset sky of dreams
Diaphanous, amber and rose.
The air is aglow with the glint and whirl
Of swift wild wings in their homeward flight,
Sapphire, emerald, topaz, and pearl,
Afloat in the evening light.

A brown quail cries from the tamarisk bushes,
A bulbul calls from the cassia-plume,
And thro' the wet earth the gentian pushes
Her spikes of silvery bloom.

Where'er the foot of the bright shower passes
Fragrant and fresh delights unfold;
The wild fawns feed on the scented grasses,
Wild bees on the cactus-gold.

An ox-cart stumbles upon the rocks,
And a wistful music pursues the breeze
From a shepherd's pipe as he gathers his flocks
Under the *pipal*-trees.
And a young *Banjara* driving her cattle
Lifts up her voice as she glitters by
In an ancient ballad of love and battle
Set to the beat of a mystic tune,
And the faint stars gleam in the eastern sky
To herald a rising moon.

The Time of Roses

Love, it is the time of roses !
In bright fields and garden closes
How they burgeon and unfold !
How they sweep o'er tombs and towers
In voluptuous crimson showers
And untrammelled tides of gold !

How they lure wild bees to capture
All the rich mellifluous rapture
Of their magical perfume,
And to passing winds surrender
All their frail and dazzling splendour
Rivalling your turban-plume !

How they cleave the air adorning
The high rivers of the morning

In a blithe, bejewelled fleet !
How they deck the moonlit grasses
In thick rainbow-tinted masses
Like a fair queen's bridal sheet !

Hide me in a shrine of roses,
Drown me in a wine of roses
Drawn from every fragrant grove !
Bind me on a pyre of roses,
Burn me in a fire of roses,
Crown me with the rose of Love !

The Peacock Lute
Songs for Music

" Iram's soft lute, with sorrow in its strings "
OMAR KHAYYAM

Silver Tears

MANY tributes Life hath brought me,
Delicate and touched with splendour . . .
Of all gracious gifts and tender
She hath given no gift diviner
Than your silver tears of Sorrow
For my wild heart's suffering.

Many evils Time hath wrought me,
Happiness and health hath broken . . .
Of all joy or grief for token
He hath left no gift diviner
Than your silver tears of Sorrow,
For my wild heart's suffering.

Caprice

You held a wild-flower in your finger-tips,
Idly you pressed it to indifferent lips,
Idly you tore its crimson leaves apart . . .
Alas! it was my heart.

You held a wine-cup in your finger-tips,
Lightly you raised it to indifferent lips,
Lightly you drank and flung away the bowl . . .
Alas! it was my soul.

Destiny

IT chanced on the noon of an April day
A dragon-fly passed in its sunward play
And furled his flight for a passing hour
To drain the life of a passion-flower. . . .
Who cares if a ruined blossom die,
O bright blue wandering dragon-fly ?

Love came, with his ivory flute,
His pleading eye, and his wingèd foot :
" I am weary," he murmured ; " O let me rest
In the sheltering joy of your fragrant breast."
At dawn he fled and he left no token. . . .
Who cares if a woman's heart be broken ?

Ashoka Blossom

IF a lovely maiden's foot
Treads on the Ashoka root,
Its glad branches sway and swell,—
So our eastern legends tell,—
Into gleaming flower,
Vivid clusters golden-red
To adorn her brow or bed
Or her marriage bower.

If your glowing foot be prest
O'er the secrets of my breast,
Love, my dreaming head would wake,
And its joyous fancies break
Into lyric bloom
To enchant the passing world
With melodious leaves unfurled
And their wild perfume.

Atonement

DEEP in a lonely garden on the hill,
    Lulled by the low sea-tides,
A shadow set in shadows, soft and still,
    A wandering spirit glides,
  Smiting its pallid palms and making moan
  O let my Love atone !

Deep in a lonely garden on the hill
    Among the fallen leaves
A shadow lost in shadows, vague and chill,
    A wandering spirit grieves,
  Beating its pallid breast and making moan
  O let my Death atone !

Longing

ROUND the sadness of my days
Breaks a melody of praise
Like a shining storm of petals,
Like a lustrous rain of pearls,
From the lutes of eager minstrels,
From the lips of glowing girls.

Round the sadness of my nights
Breaks a carnival of lights. . . .
But amid the gleaming pageant
Of life's gay and dancing crowd
Glides my cold heart like a spectre
In a rose-encircled shroud.

Love, beyond these lonely years
Lies there still a shrine of tears,

A dim sanctuary of sorrow
Where my grieving heart may rest,
And on some deep tide of slumber
Reach the comfort of your breast ?

Welcome

WELCOME, O fiery Pain !
My heart unseared, unstricken,
Drinks deep thy fervid rain,
My spirit-seeds to quicken.

Welcome, O tranquil Death !
Thou hast no ills to grieve me,
Who cam'st with Freedom's breath
From sorrow to retrieve me.

Open, O vast unknown,
Thy sealed mysterious portal !
I go to seek mine own,
Vision of Love immortal.

The Festival of Memory

DOTH rapture hold a feast,
Doth sorrow keep a fast
For Love's dear memory
Whose sweetness shall outlast
The changing winds of Time,
Secret and unsurpassed?

Shall I array my heart
In Love's vermeil attire?
O shall I fling my life
Like incense in Love's fire?
Weep unto sorrow's lute?
Dance unto rapture's lyre?

What know the world's triune
Of gifts so strange as this

I

Twin-nurtured boon of Love,
Deep agony and bliss,
Fulfilment and farewell
Concentred in a kiss?

No worship dost thou need,
O miracle divine!
Silence and song and tears
Delight and dreams are thine,
Who mak'st my burning soul
Thy sacrament and shrine.

The Temple
A Pilgrimage of Love

" My passion shall burn as the flame of Salvation,
The flower of my love shall become the ripe fruit
of Devotion "

RABINDRANATH TAGORE

I. The Gate of Delight
1. The Offering

WERE beauty mine, Beloved, I would bring it
Like a rare blossom to Love's glowing shrine ;
Were dear youth mine, Beloved, I would fling it
Like a rich pearl into Love's lustrous wine.

Were greatness mine, Beloved, I would offer
Such radiant gifts of glory and of fame,
Like camphor and like curds to pour and proffer
Before Love's bright and sacrificial flame.

But I have naught save my heart's deathless passion
That craves no recompense divinely sweet,
Content to wait in proud and lowly fashion,
And kiss the shadow of Love's passing feet.

73

2. The Feast

Bring no fragrant sandal-paste,
Let me gather, Love, instead
The entranced and flowering dust
You have honoured with your tread
For mine eyelids and mine head.

Bring no scented lotus-wreath
Moon-awakened, dew-caressed ;
Love, thro' memory's age-long dream
Sweeter shall my wild heart rest
With your foot-prints on my breast.

Bring no pearls from ravished seas,
Gems from rifled hemispheres ;
Grant me, Love, in priceless boon
All the sorrow of your years,
All the secret of your tears.

3. Ecstasy

Let spring illume the western hills with blossoming
  brands of fire,
And wake with rods of budded flame the valleys of
  the south—
But I have plucked you, O miraculous Flower of my
  desire,
And crushed between my lips the burning petals of
  your mouth !

Let spring unbind upon the breeze tresses of rich
  perfume
To lure the purple honey-bees to their enchanted
  death—
But sweeter madness drives my soul to swift and
  sweeter doom
For I have drunk the deep, delicious nectar of your
  breath !

75

Let spring unlock the melodies of fountain and of
flood,
And teach the wingèd wind of man to mock the
wild bird's art,
But wilder music thrilled me when the rivers of your
blood
Swept o'er the flood-gates of my life to drown my
waiting heart !

4. The Lute-Song

WHY need you a burnished mirror of gold,
O bright and imperious face?
Mine eyes be the shadowless wells of desire
For the sun of your glory and grace!

Why need you the praises of ivory lutes,
O proud and illustrious name?
My voice be the journeying lute of delight
For the song of your valour and fame!

Why need you pavilions and pillows of silk,
Soft foot-cloths of azure, O Sweet?
My heart be your tent and your pillow of rest,
And a place of repose for your feet!

Why need you sad penance or pardon or prayer
For life's passion and folly and fears ?
My soul be your living atonement, O Love,
In the flame of immutable years !

5. If You Call Me

If you call me I will come
  Swifter, O my Love,
Than a trembling forest deer
  Or a panting dove,
Swifter than a snake that flies
  To the charmer's thrall . . .
If you call me I will come
  Fearless what befall.

If you call me, I will come
  Swifter than desire,
Swifter than the lightning's feet
  Shod with plumes of fire.
Life's dark tides may roll between,
  Or Death's deep chasms divide—
If you call me I will come
  Fearless what betide.

6. The Sins of Love

FORGIVE me the sin of mine eyes,
O Love, if they dared for a space
Invade the dear shrine of your face
With eager, insistent delight,
Like wild birds intrepid of flight
That raid the high sanctuaried skies—
O pardon the sin of mine eyes !

Forgive me the sin of my hands . . .
Perchance they were bold overmuch
In their tremulous longing to touch
Your beautiful flesh, to caress,
To clasp you, O Love, and to bless
With gifts as uncounted as sands—
O pardon the sin of my hands !

Forgive me the sin of my mouth,
O Love, if it wrought you a wrong,
With importunate silence or song
Assailed you, encircled, oppress'd,
And ravished your lips and your breast
To comfort its anguish of drouth—
O pardon the sin of my mouth !

Forgive me the sin of my heart,
If it trespassed against you and strove
To lure or to conquer your love
Its passionate love to appease,
To solace its hunger and ease
The wound of its sorrow or smart—
O pardon the sin of my heart !

7. The Desire of Love

O could I brew my soul like wine
    To make you strong,
O could I carve you Freedom's sword
    Out of my song !

Instil into your mortal flesh
    Immortal breath,
Triumphantly to conquer Life
    And trample Death.

What starry height of sacrifice
    Were left untrod,
So could my true love fashion you
    Into a God ?

8. The Vision of Love

O Love ! my foolish heart and eyes
Have lost all knowledge save of you,
And everywhere—in blowing skies
And flowering earth—I find anew
The changing glory of your face
The myriad symbols of your grace.

To my enraptured sight you are
Sovereign and sweet reality,
The splendour of the morning star,
The might and music of the sea,
The subtle fragrance of the spring,
Rich fruit of all Time's harvesting.

O Love ! my foolish soul and sense
Have lost all vision save of you,

My sacred fount of sustenance
From which my spirit drinks anew
Sorrow and solace, hope and power
From life to life and hour to hour.

O poignant sword ! O priceless crown,
O temple of my woe and bliss !
All pain is compassed by your frown.
All joy is centred in your kiss.
You are the substance of my breath
And you the mystic pang of Death.

II. The Path of Tears
1. The Sorrow of Love

Why did you turn your face away ?
    Was it for grief or fear
Your strength would fail or your pride grow weak,
If you touched my hand, if you heard me speak,
    After a life-long year ?

Why did you turn your face away ?
    Was it for love or hate ?
Or the spell of that wild miraculous hour
That hurled our souls with relentless power
    In the eddying fires of Fate ?

Turn not your face from me, O Love !
    Shall Sorrow or Death conspire
To set our suffering spirits free
From the passionate bondage of Memory
    Or the thrall of the old desire ?

2. The Silence of Love

SINCE thus I have endowed you with the whole
Joy of my flesh and treasure of my soul,
And your life debt to me looms so supreme,
Shall my love wax ungenerous as to seem
By sign or supplication to demand
An answering gift from your reluctant hand.

Give what you will . . . if aught be yours to
     give !
But tho' you are the breath by which I live
And all my days are a consuming pyre
Of unaccomplished longing and desire,
How shall my love beseech you or beset
Your heart with sad remembrance and regret ?

Quenched are the fervent words I yearn to speak
And tho' I die, how shall I claim or seek
From your full rivers one reviving shower,
From your resplendent years one single hour?
Still for Love's sake I am foredoomed to bear
A load of passionate silence and despair.

3. The Menace of Love

How long, O Love, shall ruthless pride avail you
Or wisdom shield you with her gracious wing,
When the sharp winds of memory shall assail you
In all the poignant malice of the spring ?

All the sealed anguish of my blood shall taunt you
In the rich menace of red-flowering trees ;
The yearning sorrow of my voice shall haunt you
In the low wailing of the midnight seas.

The tumult of your own wild heart shall smite you
With strong and sleepless pinions of desire,
The subtle hunger in your veins shall bite you
With swift and unrelenting fangs of fire.

When youth and spring and passion shall betray you
And mock your proud rebellion with defeat,
God knows, O Love, if I shall save or slay you
As you lie spent and broken at my feet!

4. Love's Guerdon

FIERCE were the wounds you struck me, O my Love,
And bitter were the blows ! . . .
Sweeter from your dear hands all suffering
Than rich love-tokens other comrades bring
Of crimson oleander and of rose.

Cold was your cruel laughter, O my Love,
And cruel were your words ! . . .
Sweeter such harshness on your lips than all
Love-orisons from tender lips that fall,
And soft love-music of chakora-birds.

You plucked my heart and broke it, O my Love,
And bleeding, flung it down ! . . .
Sweeter to die thus trodden of your feet,
Than reign apart upon an ivory seat
Crowned in a lonely rapture of renown.

5. If You Were Dead

IF you were dead I should not weep !
How sweetly would my sad heart rest
Close-gathered in a dreamless sleep
Among the garlands on your breast,
Happy at last and comforted
If you were dead !

For life is like a burning veil
That keeps our yearning souls apart,
Cold Fate a wall no hope may scale,
And pride a severing sword, Sweetheart !
And love a wide and troubled sea
'Twixt you and me.

If you were dead I should not weep—
How sweetly would our hearts unite

In a dim, undivided sleep,
Locked in Death's deep and narrow night,
All anger fled, all sorrow past,
O Love, at last !

6. Supplication

Love, it were not such deep unmeasured
    wrong
To wreck my life of youth and all delight,
Bereave my days of sweetness and to blight
My hidden wells of slumber and of song,
Had your atoning mercy let me keep
For sole and sad possession to assuage
The loss of my heart's radiant heritage,
Power of such blessed tears as mortals weep.

But I, O Love, am like a withered leaf
Burnt in devouring noontides of distress
And tossed upon dim pools of weariness,
Mute to the winds of gladness or of grief.

The changing glory of the earth and skies
Kindles no answering tribute in my breast,
My loving dead go streamwards to their rest
Unhonoured by the homage of mine eyes.

Restore me not the rapture that is gone,
The hope forbidden and the dream denied,
The ruined purpose and the broken pride,
Lost kinship with the starlight and the dawn.
But you whose proud, predestined hands control
My springs of sorrow, ecstasy and power,
Grant in the brief compassion of an hour
A gift of tears to save my stricken soul !

7. The Slayer

Love, if at dawn some passer-by should say,
"Lo ! doth thy garment drip with morning dew ?
Thy face perchance is drenched with cold sea-spray,
Thy hair with fallen rain ? "
      Make answer : " *Nay,*
These be the death-drops from sad eyes I slew
With the quick torch of pain."

And if at dusk a reveller should cry,
" What rare vermilion vintage hast thou spilled,
Or is thy robe splashed with the glowing dye
Of some bruised crimson leaf ? "
      O Love reply :
" *These be the life-drops of a heart I killed*
With the swift spear of grief."

8. The Secret

THEY come, sweet maids and men with shining tribute,
Garlands and gifts, cymbals and songs of praise. . . .
How can they know I have been dead, Beloved,
These many mournful days ?

Or that my delicate dreaming soul lies trampled
Like crushed ripe fruit, chance-trodden of your feet,
And how you flung the throbbing heart that loved
    you
To serve wild dogs for meat ?

They bring me saffron veils and silver sandals
Rich crowns of honour to adorn my head—
For none save you may know the tragic secret,
O Love, that I am dead !

III. The Sanctuary
1. The Fear of Love

O COULD my love devise
A shield for you from envious lips and eyes
That desecrate the sweetness of your days
With tumults of their praise !

O could my love design
A secret, sealed, invulnerable shrine
To hide you, happy and inviolate,
From covetous Time and Fate.

Love, I am drenched with fear
Lest the uncounted avarice of the year
Add to the triumph of all garnered grace
The rapture of your face !

I tremble with despair
Lest the far-journeying winds and sunbeams bear
Bright rumours of your luring brows and breath
Unto the groves of Death.

What sanctuary can I pledge
Whose very love of you is sacrilege ?
O I would save you from the ravening fire
Of my own heart's desire !

2. The Illusion of Love

BELOVED, you may be as all men say
    Only a transient spark
Of flickering flame set in a lamp of clay—
I care not . . . since you kindle all my dark
With the immortal lustres of the day.

And as all men deem, dearest, you may be
    Only a common shell
Chance-winnowed by the sea-winds from the sea—
I care not . . . since you make most audible
The subtle murmurs of eternity.

And tho' you are, like men of mortal race,
    Only a hapless thing
That Death may mar and destiny efface—
I care not . . . since unto my heart you bring
The very vision of God's dwelling-place.

3. The Worship of Love

CRUSH me, O Love, betwixt thy radiant fingers
    Like a frail lemon leaf or basil bloom,
Till aught of me that lives for thee or lingers
    Be but the wraith of memory's perfume,
    And every sunset wind that wandereth
    Grow sweeter for my death !

Burn me, O Love, as in a glowing censer
    Dies the rich substance of a sandal grain,
Let my soul die till nought but an intenser
    Fragrance of my deep worship doth remain—
    And every twilight star shall hold its breath
    And praise thee for my death !

4. Love Triumphant

If your fair mind were quenched with dark distress,
Your dear hands stained with fierce blood-guiltiness,
Or your sweet flesh fell rotting from the bone,
Should not my deep unchanging love atone
And shield you from the sore decree of Fate
And the world's storm of horror and of hate ?

What were to me your dire disease or crime,
The scorn of men, the cold revenge of Time ?
Has life a suffering still I shall not dare,
Love, for your sake to conquer or to bear,
If I might yield you solace, succour, rest,
And hush your awful anguish on my breast ?

5. Love Omnipotent

O Love, is there aught I should fail to achieve for
    your sake ?
Your need would invest my frail hands with in-
    vincible power
To tether the dawn and the darkness, to trample and
    break
The mountains like sea-shells, and crush the fair
    moon like a flower,
And drain the wide rivers as dew-drops and pluck
    from the skies
The sunbeams like arrows, the stars like proud im-
    potent eyes.

O Love, is there aught I should fear to fulfil at your
    word ?
Your will my weak hands with such dauntless delight
    would endow

To capture and tame the wild tempest to sing like a bird,

And bend the swift lightning to fashion a crown for your brow,

Unfurl the sealed triumph of Time like a foot-cloth outspread,

And rend the cold silence that conquers the lips of the dead.

6. Love Transcendent

WHEN Time shall cease and the world be ended
And Fate unravel the judgment scroll,
And God shall hear—by His hosts attended—
The secret legend of every soul,

And each shall pass to its place appointed,
And yours to His inmost paradise,
To sit encrowned 'mid the peace-anointed,
O my saint with the sinless eyes !

My proud soul shall be unforgiven
For a passionate sin it will ne'er repent,
And I shall be doomed, O Love, and driven
And hurled from Heaven's high battlement,

Down the deep ages, alone, unfrightened,
Flung like a pebble thro' burning space ;
But the speed of my fall shall be sweet and brightened
By the memoried joy of your radiant face !

Whirled like a leaf from æon to æon,
Tossed like a feather from flame to flame,
Love, I shall chant a glorious pæan,
And thrill the dead with your deathless **name**.

So you be safe in God's mystic garden,
Inclosed like a star in **His** ageless skies,
My outlawed spirit shall crave no pardon,—
O my saint with the sinless eyes !

7. Invocation

STOOP not from thy proud, lonely sphere,
    Star of my Trust !
But shine implacable and pure,
    Serene and just ;
And bid my struggling spirit rise
    Clean from the dust !

Still let thy chastening wrath endure.
    O be thou still
A radiant and relentless flame,
    A crucible
To shatter and to shape anew
    My heart and will.

Still be thy scorn the burning height
    My feet must tread,
Still be thy grief the bitter crown
    That bows my head,
Thy stern, arraigning silences
    My daily bread !

So shall my yearning love at last
    Grow sanctified,
Thro' sorrow find deliverance
    From mortal pride,
So shall my soul, redeemed, re-born,
    Attain thy side.

8. Devotion

TAKE my flesh to feed your dogs if you choose,
Water your garden-trees with my blood if you will,
Turn my heart into ashes, my dreams into dust—
Am I not yours, O Love, to cherish or kill?

Strangle my soul and fling it into the fire!
Why should my true love falter or fear or rebel?
Love, I am yours to lie in your breast like a flower,
Or burn like a weed for your sake in the flame of hell.

PRINTED AT THE COMPLETE PRESS
WEST NORWOOD
LONDON

CPSIA information can be obtained
at www.ICGtesting.com
Printed in the USA
LVOW13*0815020718
582477LV00007B/92/P

9 780265 404041